What people are saying about

That Clear and Certain Sound

This book is like a refreshing rain—a shower of meditations on life-lessons presented so deftly and gently by the author that their true depth and breadth may at first be overlooked. Behind the clear and certain language in which Pamela Haines' voice comes across, lies a worldview deeply rooted in the Quaker ethos. Yet her stories and reflections, and the questions she ponders, will resonate with all who work to bring the healing of "right relationship" to the human world and to earth's whole commonwealth of life.

Keith Helmuth, author of *Tracking Down Ecological Guidance: Presence, Beauty, Survival*

In a world filled with lies big and little, Pamela Haines, invites us to experience truth with a capital T. Through delightful essays that ring clearly, we readers become reacquainted with an integrity and honesty that comes from the depth of the Divine. Reading these words, we are brought out of the falsehoods of this present age and encounter in hearts "that which is eternal" (George Fox).

J. Brent Bill, author of *Hope and Witness in Dangerous Times* and *Beauty, Truth, Life, and Love*

That Clear and Certain Sound stretches us "toward lives of greater connection and integrity." Simple plots of land and community gatherings seen through Pamela Haines' curious, attentive intellect reveal the rich, refreshing power in the ordinary. Her writings call us to ten̶ ̶ ̶ ̶ ̶wn lives. Reading this book to̶ ̶ ̶ ̶ ̶mily and community is a real tre̶ ̶ ̶ ̶at matter.

T0167503

Nadine Hoover, author of *Creating Cultures of Peace,* and *Discernment: Transforming Power in Daily Life*

It's hard to believe such a small book can contain so many large and useful expressions of wisdom. Pamela Haines moves effortlessly from the lessons in her garden to those found in an African village, from the creativity of young children to the inspiration adults can access to meet the climate crisis. I've rarely encountered such a profound interweaving of inward and outward challenges, with a consistent—and never facile—turn to the power of love. Her anecdotes and imagery help the insights settle in our place of recollection.

George Lakey, author of *Facilitating Group Learning*

Pamela Haines writes with heart. In a society filled with inflated grand statements and hashtag boasts, she finds nuggets of Truth tucked away in daily activity. Through her writings she brings us fundamental ways of being in community and relationship with the wide world around us. She doesn't flinch from pain or shy from exposing her failings, but allows us to be broken people looking for a way to heal and be better souls.

Daniel Hunter, author of *Strategy and Soul,* and *Building a Movement to End the New Jim Crow*

QUAKER QUICKS

That Clear and Certain Sound

Finding Solid Ground in Perilous Times

QUAKER QUICKS

That Clear and Certain Sound

Finding Solid Ground in Perilous Times

Pamela Haines

CHRISTIAN ALTERNATIVE
BOOKS

Winchester, UK
Washington, USA

JOHN HUNT PUBLISHING

First published by Christian Alternative Books, 2021
Christian Alternative Books is an imprint of John Hunt Publishing Ltd.,
No. 3 East St., Alresford, Hampshire SO24 9EE, UK
office@jhpbooks.com
www.johnhuntpublishing.com
www.christian-alternative.com

For distributor details and how to order please visit the 'Ordering' section on our website.

Text copyright: Pamela Haines 2020

ISBN: 978 1 78904 765 3
978 1 78904 766 0 (ebook)
Library of Congress Control Number: 2020947589

A CIP catalogue record for this book is available from the British Library.

Design: Stuart Davies

UK: Printed and bound by CPI Group (UK) Ltd, Croydon, CR0 4YY
Printed in North America by CPI GPS partners

We operate a distinctive and ethical publishing philosophy in all areas of our business, from our global network of authors to production and worldwide distribution.

Contents

Also by this author

Money and Soul: Quaker Faith and Practice and the Economy
978-1-78904-089-0

Preface

There was a high value placed on language when I was growing up. My mother was fascinated with the Greek and Latin roots of words, both parents appreciated the fine rules of grammar, and I learned to write a tight expository essay in high school. But the idea that the written word could be harnessed to vision, to move hearts and minds, was outside of my experience.

A seed of that possibility may have first lodged in my consciousness as a child in Quaker meeting for worship. It seemed so mysterious. You would be sitting there in the silence, not discontent, but perhaps a little disengaged. And then suddenly someone would rise to speak—someone who just moments before had been a completely ordinary adult sitting quietly with the rest of us. And I would listen, not only to the words, but to the message that had the power to propel them from the safety of their seat. I held that safety dear, and continue to prefer to sit quietly when there is an option—though I hope I have gotten braver over the years. But I wonder if something from that experience took root and shaped my attitude toward language and message.

There were disabilities around language as well. I could count on one hand the number of times our family missed going to meeting when I was growing up. At the same time, I would be hard pressed to remember even one conversation we had at home about religion. Fast forward to an attempt in middle age to communicate with a group of evangelical Quakers from Guatemala who were immigrants to Philadelphia. The opportunity to reach out across barriers of language was a compelling challenge. My Spanish is only passable, but I discovered that my real deficit was in the language of religion. That's all they were interested in talking about and I found myself inexplicably tongue tied. I had never learned to talk religion. All my training had been in the doing of it.

In the branch of Quakerism in which I was raised, there weren't that many things to believe: Truth is constantly unfolding, in continuous revelation. We are called to be in right relationship. And there is that of God in every person. Thus, the practice becomes centering in to listen for truth, reaching out for that of the divine in others, and seeking a place of right relationship—with others, with the world around us, and with the spirit that gives life to our world.

As an adult, I found myself writing—not in the tight expository style of my school years, nor in the language of theology or belief, but in reflection on these encounters in life. Sharing my reflections with a larger circle of friends and loved ones was, perhaps, my way of standing to give a message, daring to assume that what came to me as I lived my life might be of use to others. When one of them suggested that I should write a book, it occurred to me that I might already have written one.

Here then is a collection of meditations, written over the course of many years—in the non-religious language in which I'm fluent—on being alive in these wonderful and perilous times; trying to stay alert to the sound of truth even in the most unlikely places; reaching for solid ground; and stretching across barriers for the hearts of others.

1. Introduction: What Rings True

Every now and then I find myself engaged with life in a way that seems just right. I have a human interaction that is clear, connected and deeply satisfying. I soak in a moment beneath a tree, pausing to look up and take in the vibrant color and striking light and shadow. I extend the life of something old and functional with a careful mend. I do a piece of work in the world that matters, and clearly has my name on it. I take the hard next step, that's waiting to be taken, in a friendship. I use my good compost to transplant and give away a native pollinator. Something about what I'm doing rings true.

"What rings true?" This could be a powerfully illuminating question to bring to all parts of our lives. Take, for example, what we eat. Can I think of an experience with food when I sensed something deeply right? What were the ingredients that made it that way? Or take gift-giving. When has a moment in that emotionally-charged minefield rung true? What made it right? When has my mind been clear? When have I had an interaction, no matter how simple, that I'd be happy to live over and over again? What made that possible?

A bell can't ring true when it is covered or padded or stuffed. To hear the ring of truth in our lives, it can help to strip down. What clutters our minds? What messages have we taken in—from our childhoods, from advertising, from society at large—that muffle the truth? What has accreted to our social institutions that keeps us from discerning their true vocations? What layers of history, privilege and inequality obscure the possibility of respectful and appreciative interaction in any situation?

I treasure the words of John Woolman, a colonial Quaker. He advises us to "Dig deep,... carefully cast forth the loose matter and get down to the rock, the sure foundation, and there hearken to the Divine Voice which gives a clear and certain sound." What if the central principle for organizing our lives was moving ever closer to what rings true?

It can be discouraging to notice how much of our time is spent elsewhere. We know what we're doing doesn't ring true, but it's hard to see an alternative. Or we try to get some relief from that tinny sound with activities that are supposed to be pleasurable or comforting, but then those activities — often some form of addictive behavior — don't quite ring true either. The relief doesn't really satisfy, and it's hard to know where to turn.

Just identifying this as something we want, however, and being able to recognize the moments when we've had it, is a big step forward. I smile as I imagine us counting up the minutes that ring true in our lives — just two minutes this day, maybe seven the next — and then reaching for more.

I think of a wise friend who is gifted with parents and children. The times that are truly golden, she says, come when you've played with a child in enough different ways that you can find a spot where they laugh openly and freely — then you stay at that spot, and they laugh and laugh. We don't have to just wait for a miracle to hear the ring of truth more often in our lives. We can remember those moments, and value them. We can look for where they most reliably happen. We can talk with our friends, and get help working to reproduce the conditions that encourage them. We can dig away at the stuff that muffles them. There may be no work that's harder — or more worth doing. And maybe, as we keep trying, it will get less hard — and we'll hear that ring of truth in our lives more and more.

2. Windows and Reflections

Sacred spaces

I wanted a support group for women I had met through my job with childcare workers—a group that would cross barriers of class and race, where women could listen deeply to each other and be supported in moving forward with life goals.

I made my invitations. I spent time cleaning so the environment would be welcoming. I left work early to be unrushed and fully present. I brought fresh mint from my garden for the ice water. My friend brought flowers. I talked about the precious gift of listening that we can give each other. I set up moments for us each to appreciate that gift. Reflecting on all these things, I realize that I was creating a sacred space, building a container for an experience that was more centered than our ordinary day-to-day lives.

During that same time, I had been grieving over the ending of a three-week kayaking vacation with a precious homemade extended family. The defining element of that experience was the irresistible invitation to be fully present with and open to those people and the environment around us. It was a sacred space.

For many of us, a religious service is the container for such a space. It provides rest and refreshment, while anchoring us in goodness. I'm still learning to do the preparation as an individual member that helps keep the container strong. And we all have much to learn about extending that container beyond the sanctuary itself.

As I notice my desire to create more of that kind of space in my daily life, other pieces fall into place. It took me a while to realize the role I've played in a small family group in my Quaker meeting, in creating and holding such a container— being present, centered and welcoming. I think of the discipline

I try to use on the trolley. When I remember to offer a silent prayer of blessing for each person as they get on, my life goes better. And then there are all the times I give someone my full and undivided attention, focused on reaching for the very best in them.

After realizing what I had been doing very methodically and intentionally (if subconsciously) with my support group, and in these other ways, a question came up at work about the monthly gathering of our childcare workers' economic justice campaign. We had been experimenting with different forms — straight business, training, social hour — and hadn't quite gotten it right. What would it mean to make that a sacred space? I would have to be more intentional. It would require stepping out of the busy/work/task mode and focusing on being relaxed and fully present to each person. I think it could be done; I think it would make a difference.

Now that I get the concept, I see the potential for so much more. I'm left wondering if there's any limit. At home, with family or dishes, at work, with friends, on the street — where are the unformed sacred spaces waiting to be called into being?

Help and confidence

Something had happened to my computer, leaving me unable to get on the Internet. Nothing I tried made a difference, except possibly to make it worse. Nobody around me could help. The computer store seemed to offer the only hope.

I had never gotten tech help there, and couldn't quite believe there wasn't some catch. I'm generally suspicious of institutional bureaucracies, and of putting myself in the hands of people with power. I would rather stay away, but there seemed to be no alternative.

So, I walk into the store with my unusable computer, my story, my need, and my suspicion. What I get is a revelation: pure help, served up with kindness on all sides. It takes two visits, but I leave with a system that is not only restored but improved, and a head swirling with new thoughts and images about help.

Why is this experience still reverberating after days? Well, help is something that I struggle with in general. I'm used to not asking for it, not getting it, assuming it's not there, managing on my own. So, this was a striking reminder that my habits and assumptions come from deep in the past and are neither the best fit for current reality nor the best prescription for my emotional well-being.

But there's more. What was it that allowed all the staff in this store — and I interacted with many of them over those two days — to offer their help with such warmth and generosity? While good customer service training may play a role, I can't believe it explains the whole. I think the key lies in the fact that they knew they could help. We were coming in with problems that had solutions; we didn't have access to those solutions, but they did. They could afford to be kind, because they were confident. And they had each other. When one part of the puzzle I brought in was outside someone's expertise, he was totally relaxed about letting me know that he needed to consult. He wasn't worried about the outcome, or about his self-worth. He didn't try to make what he knew be enough when it wasn't. He didn't need to defend his limitations or worry about them. He knew that together they could do anything that was possible to be done.

I begin imagining other things that might be fixed in such an environment. Maybe children could bring their malfunctioning families to the store. They would describe the problem they were experiencing and an employee would say, "Oh yes, we can help you with this. We know what to do. We've seen this problem before. It may take a little while, but we can straighten it out."

Or maybe people who are concerned about the climate

could bring the planet to the store. They would explain what was broken, and an employee would say, "You're right; this is a bad problem. I'll have to call in all my colleagues—and actually there's a role you'll need to play here too. Let me explain the process. It will take quite a while, but don't worry. We do know just what has to be done."

As these scenarios were finding a home in my brain, I started wondering about the times that people come to me for help. Do they see me the way I saw that staff, as unwaveringly confident, kind and able? That's a pretty humbling thought! While I do try to be kind, I often don't feel all that confident, and there are lots of problems I can't solve. But I see the importance of sharing every bit of real confidence I do have. And when I lack it, maybe that's where my co-workers—my fellow human beings—come in. What would it mean, and what would it make possible, if we all could rest in the confidence that we have each other, and that together we can do anything that is possible to be done?

Spending and saving

I struggle at my little plot at the community garden with waiting too long to harvest my vegetables. I'm always waiting for them to grow just a little bit bigger, or saving them for later when I might need them more. But if I wait too long, they get bitter or tough, or fall off the vine. It's particularly hard in the spring, when everything edible that's made it through the winter seems like a miracle. You don't want to just gobble up your miracles!

I'm not a big spender in general, while I'm a very good saver, so I guess this attitude toward the garden shouldn't surprise me. But it really doesn't make sense. As I promise myself this year to pick generously and go for the goal of using everything up, I find myself pondering the larger question of spending and saving. Are there other things that are better spent than saved?

Clearly, for starters, there is our time. One of the problems with all the emphasis in our culture on time-saving technology is that it offers no help in making wise decisions about spending it. Yet if we don't choose to spend our time today, it's wasted and gone.

When we think about our energy, spending often has a negative connotation. We have expended too much energy, or our energy is spent. Conservation is seen as wise. True, it's not good to push our bodies beyond their capacity, or deny them rest when they have been assaulted and need to recover. But in a way, our energy is like our time. If we don't make choices about how to spend today's supply, it's gone forever.

Then there is caring. Again, the inclination to be protective and spend it cautiously is strong. We want to put our caring into safe investments, where we can count on it yielding good returns. This is understandable, given how often it has been abused, starting when we were very young. But from another perspective, it is our nature to care, and withholding today will not increase the amount we have for tomorrow. If we can get access to that well of natural caring, there is an endless supply (though we'll probably have to grieve as well, to keep the channels clear). We can care hugely, every day, and there will still be the same amount left.

Money may be the hardest. Good arguments can be made for both spending and saving. But I wonder, if we put our attention to being big spenders in other ways—in time and energy and caring—maybe the money choices will be easier to sort out.

In the meantime, I plan to harvest this season with more thought to the present. Yes, I'll try to spread out the season and think about what can be preserved. But then I'll pick my vegetables when they are new and when they are in their prime and not wait. I'll use them up—enjoying each mouthful—and put my faith in the seeds' and the land's ability to produce again.

Right to repair

When my old computer needed a new battery, it was incredibly frustrating to have that simple repair unavailable to me. We routinely buy new phones because repair would cost more than the phone itself. I'm ready to join the movement for a basic right to repair!

I know what it's like to make a good repair and extend the life of something that has value through my time and skill. Sometimes it's as simple as sewing back a button on a shirt or a favorite pair of jeans. Stitching up a seam to make a beloved stuffed animal as good as new can take just a few minutes, but bring joy to a child. When we found an old chest on the street—wobbly and falling apart in many ways—glue and clamps were really all that were needed to make it a lovely and desirable piece of furniture again. Our grandchildren are entranced by the possibility, and the process, of fixing broken toys. They are clear about the joy and power of repair.

I also know what it is like to find a good repair person who can pick up where my skills left off. These relationships are priceless, and am never quite comfortable with a new appliance till I find someone who can keep it going. It was a pleasure to get to know the man who was so good with our washer, dryer and stove, resting in the knowledge that I was in the very best of hands. I'll never forget the sewing machine repair man who once sent home not only my repaired machine, but another one that he had on hand and thought I could use! I have a deep respect for the skills of such people, and my life is better for knowing them.

What would it mean to have a right to repair? If manufacturers produced with the sustainability of products and the planet in mind, it would not only cut down waste, extend product life, slow global warming and support a cadre of skilled repair people; it would reorient our whole culture to one of valuing what we have rather than focusing always on the next new thing.

Maybe it would invite us to think even more broadly about repair. Just as those who are already skilled in repair take pride in their craft, maybe we could become a whole culture of repairers. What if we believed that we could build the skills to repair other things that are broken—broken relationships, broken communities, broken economic systems?

Of course, some things should never be produced in the first place, and some are simply beyond repair. But maybe if we set our repair sights higher, we could expand the categories of things we don't throw away—to include phones, computers, washers, refrigerators, small towns, marginalized people. To repair assumes agency and power. What if we claimed it as a human right?

When more is less

In stories of the old days, we read of different rare delights: the first greens after a long winter, the miracle of an orange, brand new shoes of one's own, a trip to town. We can almost taste the pleasure of such moments—the exquisite experience of luxury.

Yet those pleasures are no longer ours. A trip to town doesn't even score as an event in most people's awareness. New shoes and oranges are nice, but hardly an occasion to feel blessed. The idea of a winter without lettuce is unthinkable, and we'd probably turn up our noses at those dandelion greens—or whatever—that our forebears were so thrilled to eat.

Are we better off? In some ways, perhaps. Yet when abundance breeds entitlement, we are the losers.

I go to our community garden plot in the midst of the city and pick the first few little strawberries and feel like the luckiest person in the world. Then my husband loads up on big fat transcontinental berries from the grocery store and my paltry little handful loses all its value. I'm at a loss. Do I want to impose scarcity on my family? How can I help us be thankful in the midst of so much?

When we joined a Community Supported Agriculture project, it was fun to walk the city streets swinging a basket of produce from the farm, but I was surprised when we stopped getting lettuce in July. The farmers said it was too hot for lettuce. I noticed how put off I felt by their inability to produce. Yet what, exactly, makes me entitled to lettuce?

When we move from appreciating something as a rare luxury, to taking it for granted, to feeling ill-used without it, there is a steady loss of pleasure. Our ability to be thankful is diminished.

I think I would be happier if I didn't feel entitled to lettuce. I think my family would be better off if we didn't take California strawberries for granted.

Language learning

People talk about the value of growing up in a bi-lingual family, but this was something else. As the story goes, Maximilian Berlitz (of language school fame) had an extended family with a rich mixture of ethnicities, and many different languages were spoken around him. When he was very little, he thought that everybody spoke their own individual language, and if you wanted to communicate with them, you had to learn it. So, he did. The way I heard the story, he was not overwhelmed or upset by this situation; it was just a fact of life.

I was recently with a group of people discussing the challenge of communicating across religious language barriers. If you and I don't have a religious language in common, it's hard to communicate. I think this is true of political and values language as well. And it's particularly confusing when we think we're speaking the same language, using the same words but mean different things by them.

Perhaps that little boy has something to teach us. Maybe before I start making easy assumptions about what you are saying, I need to consider that I don't know your language.

Maybe I need to stop and do a lot of listening (as I'm sure he did) and ask questions so I can hear your words in many different contexts and sort out what a comparable word in my language might be.

Maybe I need to ask the question, "What will allow me to understand you?" It's hard to be around language we don't understand, hard to feel drawn toward others whose words we can't make sense of. Yet, rather than seizing on the signs that the chasms are too deep to ever be crossed, maybe we can stay in learning/translating mode, waiting and doing the work that will allow us to move toward the other person. Wouldn't it be wonderful to have the confidence of little Maximilian Berlitz — that we can learn any language, decipher any human being?

Home-made play

I had offered to do childcare for a group of mostly childless young adults, and it turned out that there was just one five-year-old boy — and no toys. So, we went to the kitchen to give the grown-ups as much space as possible, and found the recycling bin under the kitchen table. We began exploring its contents: an egg carton, a yoghurt container, a tuna fish can, one of those little plastic cups that sauces and dressings for fast food come in, its lid, and the foil of a candy wrapper.

We settled in on the floor and started by building towers, trying different arrangements with the containers, and noticing what was the same and what was different. I discovered that if we opened the egg carton a little and put it on end, we could make a tall building. He checked out the foil, announcing that it had been milk chocolate. Though I had never considered that you could smell the difference in chocolates, as I sniffed, I had to agree. Noticing the strength of the smell, he speculated that it had been blueberry — one of his favorite foods.

He began making meteorites from the foil, and it was surprising to see how they shook the tower, but didn't knock it down. Then the meteorites transformed into a lumpy monster, putting an (imaginary) passerby in danger. But the monster bumped into the leg of the table, and we discovered that it was because the light hurt his eyes and he had to close them when he walked. He tried again, got bumped again, and died. This monster, whom I had grown fond of as his vulnerabilities became apparent, transformed into another monster, this time with a long saber and a distinct head that looked up and down. Then it grew a tail and transformed into a dinosaur. A tiny bit of foil that I had put in the little lid on the top of the building became a dinosaur egg, and the lid became a nest. The dinosaur, which changed fluidly from ankylosaurus to tyrannosaurus rex, showed an amazing ability to leap over tall buildings. Several times our tower got knocked down, but luckily, I was able to rebuild it each time.

We had been happily engaged together for about an hour, and had by no means exhausted the possibilities of this play, when his mom came to find us in the kitchen and take him home to bed. So, we disassembled the tower and put all the recyclables back in the bin, except for the foil, which was turning into another dinosaur in his busy hands—way too valuable a plaything to be abandoned.

I found this short time together on the kitchen floor both totally enjoyable and vastly reassuring. We had nothing that could remotely resemble a toy, much less anything that required external power or involved a screen. Yet what we had was enough. That a twenty-first-century child from the United States could create such rich and flexible play from these homely ingredients was enormously hopeful. It was a sign: that the initiative and creativity of the next generation have not been permanently stunted by our society's addiction to consumption and the purchase of entertainment, and that it's possible to downsize without sacrificing life's essential pleasures.

As I think of this experience and other home-made pleasures, a big game of Capture the Flag in the park or a neighborhood gathering to sing Handel's Messiah, I see them as acts of cultural revolution. They create a precious space, where it is possible to breathe deeply. Finding such space these days can be like pulling barbed wire from around our bodies, scraping grime off our eyes. We all need it. Our children are dying for it. It is worthy of our time, our energy, our creativity, our priority. It is a profound expression of humanity, and hope for the future.

Interior decorating

I love the long December evening each year when we gather at a friend's house, pack into every space in the living and dining rooms, and pour ourselves into bringing the Messiah to life. I'm filled up with beautiful music, and it's one of those gifts that keeps on giving; the music makes its home inside my head and I keep hearing it for days. Reflecting on what a good choice this had been about what I want in my head, I start to consider how else I can pay attention to that interior space.

I already think about the movies, books, and TV I consume with an eye toward what will remain in my head. What scenes and words, what kinds of assumptions about human nature and the world we live in, would I like to have linger?

I remember wise things that I've heard about this "There is both a wolf and a dove inside each of us. Which will grow? The one that is fed." "Hanging on to resentment is like giving yourself poison and hoping the other person will die." It's been heartening to discover that when I start down a path of resentment inside my head these days, I can often notice it happening, remember that I don't want to go there, and get back on a path of my own choosing. My inside space is so much cleaner as a result.

Then there's the question of other things I might want to add to that space, to make it an even more inviting place to live. In a children's book I came across recently, a child says, "Dad believes that the things of nature are a gift. And that in return, we must give something back. We must give thanks." My day goes better when I remember to be thankful for the sky and the earth as I walk down the street. My commute goes better when I offer a loving thought to each person who gets on the trolley.

When I focus my attention more on what inclines me toward hope, and less on what tips me toward despair, it's easier to think well about what to do. It's like there's less stuff lying around inside to trip me up. (And while I may need to look straight at despair at times, I always know where to find it.)

This way of thinking puts housekeeping and interior decorating in a whole new light. While I'm not that particular about my external house furnishings, I realize that I care deeply about the space inside my head. I would choose to create plenty of space and light, and to clean out everything that obscures my vision and hinders me from acting with love and power in the present.

3. Love and Grief

On love and grief

What do we do with all that is wrong in our world? My personal strategy over many years has been to focus on what is right, and put my energy toward helping it grow. This has certainly made my life better—and probably the lives of others as well. Yet an exclusive focus on the good and the possible is feeling a little tight and frayed these days. In a way, it has always been a protection. I can't quite bear to really take in all that is not right. I know a great deal about it, and care deeply. My choices have been framed by that knowledge, but I've kept it at arm's length. I've been unwilling to have a life shaped by rage and despair; unwilling to join in charges of evil that seem to just stereotype, blame, and separate; unwilling to carry the burden of the world. I haven't known another way to interact with, to contain, the depth of what is wrong.

Yet a voice inside me is getting louder and more insistent— we need to grieve. As a parent I've championed children's right to grieve. Though we want to step in and make everything better, there are some things we just can't fix. If, at these times, we can wrench our attention away from solutions and just help them grieve, they have an incredible capacity to bounce back to face life's next challenge.

After all, no one can heal without grieving their loss. The search for easier or more comfortable alternatives just seems to lead to more pain—payback, vengeance, the death penalty, bombs. How can our world heal without a much larger outpouring of grief—not just the sum of many individuals grieving individual loss, but grief for the world as a whole?

This poor old world is getting lots of action fueled by anger and outrage—and lots of inaction held in place by despair. Yet what are anger and despair but indicators of aborted grieving?

Anger makes us quick to find enemies, and its fires burn us as well. Despair knocks us out of the public arena, sends us on the quest for personal happiness, makes us vulnerable to consumerism, addictions, the need for entertainment, and belief systems that hold us separate or uninvolved. Seeking a life of individual purity, to minimize or make amends for personal complicity, may be laudable but it doesn't get at the whole. There is certainly lots of action based in love as well—and we need all of it that we can get—but there is not much big open-hearted grief.

Somehow, with attention on the need to grieve (and with a faith that I am supported by a force for good alive and moving in this world), I find myself more willing to engage with the evil that I've refused to focus on all my life.

There is some intimate connection between evil-doing, oppression and grief. What if hardness of heart is an indication of the need for tears of grief to soften that hard shell? Does the end of oppression require the grief of those who oppress? While I may not do much evil directly, we are all caught in the coils of oppression. Just being citizens of a rich nation ensures that. None of us are free, none are uninvolved.

We can work to change the forces of evil and domination and oppression. There are hundreds of ways, all valid, all important. Maintaining hope, and acting in line with our truest beliefs, is part of what makes our lives complete. But we need more than work. We need to be present to all that is wrong as we love what could be. We need to be overwhelmed with open-hearted grief as we turn toward healing and change. If those who traffic most directly in injustice cannot yet grieve, then perhaps I can. Perhaps my tears, the tears of all of us, can help in the healing of weary evil doers as well as those who suffer under their hands. As we find ways to grieve—and grieve together— perhaps new paths we had never imagined will open before us.

Swimming in the same sea

When I was growing up, there was a pond nearby, and everyone in the neighborhood came to the pond to swim. Then, as an adult, I can remember looking from an airplane at housing developments spread out below, almost every one with its little dot or squiggle of blue in the back—the swimming pool. What we used to do in public, in common water, we now did separately, through our own resources, on our own property. Swimming was becoming more and more individualized and privatized.

With a devastating earthquake dominating the news one winter, I felt that I ought to be grieving more deeply for so much terrible loss. As I looked for excuses, they were there to be found: our family was still reeling from a beloved grandmother's debilitating stroke; a treasured mentor—a giant of a man—had just died; a cherished hope that a loved one would come home had to be laid to rest. I was filled up with my own sorrows. There just didn't seem to be space for any more.

While there was weight and truth to all of this, it didn't satisfy. It left me too much on my own, too separated from the folks in Haiti, too disconnected from the larger world. As I was reaching for a framework that I could live with, the image of a great common sea came to mind. What if I didn't have to think of all these troubles as my own private little pool of grief. What if I could leave my backyard and come out to the sea with everyone else who was grieving all the loss of the world? Those impossible questions, "Why me?" and "Why them instead of me?" might lose some of their sting in the recognition that it's all ours.

It's not that we want any of it. It would seem that a person could save a lot of heartache by choosing to just stay out of the water altogether, passing up both private pool and common sea. Many of us put considerable effort into creating lives that skirt the edges of heartache. We decide not to look, not to take things in. We close our eyes when it seems like too much. But the price of hardening our hearts is high, and ultimately, we don't have control. A loved one is snatched away and we find ourselves drowning. Or the image of a single desolate child in the news slips through our defenses and into our unprepared hearts. Somehow, I think that if we come to terms with the reality that we are going to be swimming in these waters whether we choose to or not, then we can learn to swim well. And if we come to the common sea, if my tears can flow in with the tears of those who lost so much in Haiti, then we can be bound together in our loss.

Maybe it's really all the same grief. Maybe that string of personal losses just loosened my share of the tears of the world. Maybe those tears flowing down my cheeks are mine to feel, but not mine to possess or control, not mine to ascribe to this particular loss or that one.

The same would have to hold true for love. It's easy to think of our loves as private affairs. But what if there's a great sea of love that we all get to swim in? Any loving that I do, then, is part of the great loving of the world. I'm left thinking that who we can grieve for and who we can love is less important than whether we are willing to step into that common sea, and do the big loving and grieving that our world needs.

Listen and love

Over lunch at a workshop for families in Tanzania, we were talking about how to break the pattern of harsh treatment of children which has been so much a part of the culture there. One man asked a question about a specific issue with a specific child. Though I have a lot of experience working with families, of course I didn't have an answer for him. It depended so much on their relationship, his intentions, and his ability to do things as a parent that he had never experienced as a child. So, I responded that a child who feels loved will forgive many mistakes, and that the solution lies within that parent. He just needs enough loving attention to help peel away all the layers of hurt that cover that solution up.

There are so many answers we didn't have, so many problems we couldn't solve. Unmet material needs there are enormous and heartbreaking, and the change in political and economic systems that is required to really make a difference will only come from a great gathering of changed hearts and empowered communities—both in Africa and the West.

But I can do my share. I can listen and love and grieve. I can pay attention, be as present as I know how, and be alert for my best role in each new moment—as both giver and receiver, in ways both large and small.

And so we listen and we love, strengthening a network of connections and our common capacity to help each other peel away the layers of hurts that obscure our loving powerful selves and the solutions that lie within. I am reminded of the advice of theologian Walter Wink: to attend to listening for what is ours to do in this world, then to do just that—no less and no more—and wait in modest confidence for a miracle.

For love of the land

I've loved this bit of land for over fifty years. Coming up over the hill, my heart always opens anew to the jewel of a valley spread out below, part of the rolling farmland and woodlots of central New York state. My father bought an old farm here in the sixties, preparing for a job move that didn't work out. But my family loved the land. The old farmhouse became a focal point for a group of young adult Quakers, a gathering and landing place as we attempted to shape lives that aligned with our deepest faith values. Our community loved the land.

Then my mother moved up there in her retirement and it became the center of family gatherings for her six children and growing extended family. My sister lived across the road on adjoining farmland, and dug her roots in deep. When my mother died, it took us some time to decide that we needed to sell the house, but none of us wanted to sell the land. How could we ensure that it would continue to be loved as we loved it?

My sister had been on her own journey, building ever-closer relationships with members of the neighboring Onondaga nation, and coming under the weight of our country's history of broken treaties, stolen land, and destruction of whole indigenous nations. Living on traditional Oneida territory, she had started exploring the idea of a land trust with the Haudenosaunee Confederacy (who used to be known as the Iroquois) of which the Oneida are a part. But as time passed with no visible progress, the outcome seemed increasingly uncertain.

Then, last fall she met an Oneida woman who was working with other Oneida in Wisconsin and southern Ontario to rekindle a shared traditional identity—a challenge, given that the only tiny remnant of their traditional homeland was now given over to a casino and entertainment complex. This meeting was the opening my sister had been waiting and hoping for. Over the next nine months, they worked together to create a nonprofit organization, my sister consulted with her siblings, and we joyfully agreed to return that thirty acres to these Oneida women.

At a ceremony the next summer, the three groups of Oneida women gathered on the land to mark its return. They sang to the land in its home language. They squished their toes in the wet earth. I can't imagine any better resolution, any better future for that land that so many of us have loved over all these years— and so many Oneida people had loved long before.

I was already struggling to take in the terrible injustice of our nation's treatment of native people. But being able to be part of one tiny thing that was so completely right has opened me up in a new way—both to the heartbreak and to the possibilities of healing.

In focus

There is something about being in a very different culture that gives the connections one is able to make—across great differences in life experience—an extra sweetness and poignancy. My relationship with one young man in Northern Uganda stands out. Somehow, we were able to find each other. You could call it a miracle. None of the host of forces that can so easily block one human being's access to another was able to prevail. Without the distractions and assumptions of daily life at home, I was reaching for connection and ready to see. After years as an orphan, being treated as an inconvenience and a burden, he was more than ready to be seen. The love in two hearts found a way to flow clear and unobstructed, as refreshing as good water in parched earth.

I believe it was a miracle, as it continues to be. And I am starting to believe that such miracles are waiting to be found at every turn. Just as this young man came into clear focus for me, in all his goodness and worth, I think there's a way that we would all choose to see and be seen. The key is to bring our loving attention to the challenge of focusing in on the reality of another human being.

So, what does it mean to see people in focus? Perhaps the better question is what gets in our way? Sometimes we just don't see at all. Our attention may be focused so far out, on the great mysteries or evils of the world, that the people close in around us are just a blur. Conversely, our attention may be focused so deep within, on our own internal state, that we can't really see anybody outside of ourselves clearly. In neither case is our focus on the people in our midst, and we catch glimpses of them only by chance.

Sometimes we are ready to focus at that range but, rather than putting attention to what is actually happening for the person in front of us, we look to see a reflection of what we want or need. This often happens with babies. In our eagerness to take in a vision of precious innocence and sweetness that nourishes our souls, we may totally miss seeing that individual human being and what they are showing on their own behalf. Or we look at a potential romantic partner, not as he or she actually is, but as a reflection of our own hopes and dreams.

We may know that there's a real live person in front of us whom we could theoretically look at, but just not be able to face what we would see if we looked. Maybe they are hurting too much for us to know how to take it in. Maybe we feel inadequate in response to their needs. Maybe they remind us of our failings, or call out anger that we don't know how to control. So we blur our vision intentionally or turn away.

Sometimes, our intention is to be present and have the other person in focus, but we're trying to do other things at the same time. This can easily happen to parents, trying to catch enough of the drift of what a child is doing or saying that we can respond appropriately, as we try at the same time to attend to another task. Or we converse with somebody while our minds are being tugged by our cell phones or our worries or by somebody else who is in the room.

All of these are real challenges. But I'm finding myself taken by the power of what can happen when we choose to not be limited by them, and dare to put our full attention to the person in front of us. Being seen that way, in full focus, will surely be a gift to them. For some it will be another always welcome affirmation that they have been seen. For others it may be life-changing, like the water on dry earth that allows a struggling plant to bloom.

But perhaps more important, really seeing others is a gift to us. (I remember going into cataract surgery with vision in one eye so cloudy that I couldn't distinguish faces and coming out to find the world crystal clear. Talk about miracles!) Though it may be painful, and may require us to grieve, ultimately seeing calls out our love. And that means more love, not only out in the world, but at our disposal in our hearts.

Sharing a tattered world

Her world is in tatters. Her loved ones are threatened. By some miracle she finds herself relatively whole. So, she has this day to work and love and knit together the fabric of her world as best she can.

I had in my heart a particular grandmother who lived not far from me and had been in the news. Some of her children had been lost to drugs. One had been killed, another accused in a killing. In a neighborhood ravaged by crime, she was now raising a granddaughter, trying against all odds to keep her safe. She seemed the only whole person in the picture. How could she keep going amidst such violence and despair? And how could she and I ever have anything in common?

I've had difficulty knowing how to deal with the ease of my life. How can it be that I've been spared so many difficulties that others face day in and day out—war, poverty, the heavy hand of injustice? I did not choose that ease, and it seems to disconnect me, distance me from so much of the rest of the world. I would not choose war, poverty or injustice either, but I grieve for those who carry such a heavy burden, and know how untested my strength and courage have been.

It came to me in sudden clarity that, despite all this, we were just the same. That grandmother's world was in tatters. My world was in tatters. Not my immediate life, my family and neighborhood, but my larger life. My city was poor, my schools struggling. My country that I loved promoted grave injustice. Brothers and sisters in other countries lived in terrible need. Some of them did unspeakable things to each other. Our common environment unraveled.

By some miracle, amidst the wreckage of her world this grandmother is still standing, still able to think and work and love. It is the same with me. I have done nothing to deserve it, yet I too find myself standing, relatively whole.

Of course I could choose to tell the story another way. I could define my world smaller—small enough to include only those who live in ease. I could wall out everything else as something alien, not part of me. There would be comfort, of a sort, in feeling no connection to poverty, injustice, war, no connection to this grandmother.

But I find the other story more profoundly reassuring. True, it means knowing things about the world that are pleasanter not to know, and claiming them as part of my life. It means stretching to find ways to love beyond my little circle of family and friends. It means working to mend the torn spots that I can reach. But it leaves me part of the whole.

In the details, my daily tasks and challenges might be very different from those of that grandmother, or of any other survivor. Nor can I pretend that a history of racial and economic injustice doesn't weigh heavily on us all and hinder our ability to find our way to each other. But in the larger sense, we are just the same. Our world is in tatters. Our loved ones are threatened. By some miracle we find ourselves standing. So, we have this day to work and love and knit together the fabric of our world as best we can.

4. Separation and Belonging

On being rooted

An okra seed had sprouted at the very edge of the plot—
vulnerable to being trampled. I decided to transplant it to more
hospitable ground. I dug it up with a good clump of earth around
the roots, settled it in a new spot, gave it a good watering and
covered it with a big pot to protect it from the sun and the hard
work of photosynthesis, while it adjusted to the move.

This will often be enough. But when I checked the next day,
the leaves were drooping, so I gave it more water. The next day
it looked perky again, as good as new, so I took off the pot. Later
I found it wilted, gave it more water and covered it up again.
Still later, I looked and found that one of the two main leaves
had dried, but the second one was holding up. This okra plant,
while still alive, was not responding well to being transplanted.
I can't say that I blame it. Who likes being yanked out of the
place where they have their roots?

Not long afterward I had the privilege of spending a day
soaking up the perspective of a man from the Basque Country.
Divided between Spain and France, the Basque people have
an ancient language and a fierce sense of shared identity. His
description of his family clans and their totems—the wolf,
and the fir that stands in stony ground—opened up a new
understanding that indigenous culture may be found in many
places.

His message was that the more we can hold onto—or
reclaim—our original language, our sense of place, our roots,
the more able we will be to act from a place of connection and
power in the present.

There's something about this that makes intuitive sense.
Being rooted can buffer us against the impact of big impersonal
social forces. If we're all floating free, a mass of undifferentiated

27

individuals with no more sense of connection to one place or set of people than another, then it's easy to be swept along in the currents of the latest thing, easy to be used in the service of an uncaring and manipulative global culture and economy.

On the other hand, a narrow cultural identity can be limiting. There is value in being able to set aside differences to claim a larger common identity: as Americans, as global citizens. And for those who have been uprooted from their home cultures and can't go back, it's important to put care into the process of transplanting, doing what's necessary to put down strong and healthy roots in new ground.

Yet we are so ready to move—to pursue opportunities, to explore new places, to endlessly reinvent ourselves, to find our support in a vast and fluid network of cyber-connections. In a way we haven't gotten over being settlers, always on the move in search of the next great frontier. To choose to stay in place seems like a character flaw—unambitious, lacking in vision.

What would it mean internally to stop being settlers, and start learning to be native to a place and its people? What would we have to give up—and what would be gained—by deciding to "bloom where we are planted"? Is there a lost language of the heart that, if recovered, would ease some tight internal place and allow for new possibilities we haven't even imagined?

Perhaps this is our next great frontier: reclaiming the value of cultural heritage and language, learning the many different ways to be grounded within our identities, and perfecting the art of putting down roots.

Bringing what we have

One thing about spending two weeks in a poor and oppressed part of a poor African country that has endured twenty years of brutal civil war is that you see a lot of hard things. And one thing about inviting people from such a community to build their skills in telling and listening to each other's stories is that you hear a lot of hard stories.

It can be confusing to know where to stand. On the one hand, the opportunity to be together is precious, and clearly a gift for everyone involved. On the other hand, my husband and I had the luxury of going back home to comfortable lives in a rich country, while they are left to live with fierce scarcity and uncertain futures.

This is a common experience, repeated tens of thousands of times as westerners venture out to Asia, Latin America and Africa, meet new people, fall in love, come up against the realities of poverty and inequality — and then go home. We want to help. But I've become increasingly aware of the many traps that come with people who have more trying to help people who have less.

One way to get those traps more clearly into focus is to check my motivation, and ask myself who and what is at the center of my helping story? If I'm helping you in order to relieve my guilt, and I need your cooperation to succeed, then the heart of the story is about me. If I'm helping you in order to confirm my generosity, and you are a necessary part of that picture, then again, the story is about me. If I'm helping you in order to expand my influence and good works, and I can't do it without you, then the story is still about me.

We may be able to accomplish things that are of use to other people with these as our underlying — and often unconscious — motivations. But there's a distortion. My gift has strings attached; I need something back. I need your lives to improve so I can feel less guilty. I need your thanks so I can feel generous. I need the project to grow so I can feel influential. On the surface it may look like it's all about your needs, but, really, it's a whole lot about mine.

Over the years I've developed a sensitivity to these traps — and am more likely to fall into one all the way at the other end of the spectrum: Since what I have is so clearly inadequate in the face of what you need, I should do us both a favor and keep my distance.

Now wary of that trap as well, I've been trying on a new point of view for my life in general, and carried it with me on our trip. What I bring clearly isn't enough. It won't come near to solving your problems. But it's all I have, and I want to be with you. I'd rather face what feels like complete inadequacy than give up on the possibility of being close. Somehow, this focus on choosing for connection and bringing what I have leads me to solid ground.

What we brought to Northern Uganda fell far short of the need we encountered there. We didn't bring enough money to begin to make a difference. We didn't have enough understanding of the local situation to be able to suggest viable income generating activities. We hadn't done enough advance work to line up meetings between local players who might be resourceful to each other. We weren't there long enough to follow through on opportunities that arose. How could this possibly be enough?

Yet we brought what we had. We did some income sharing with our friend. With the group that had gathered around, we shared everything we knew about peer listening that could help in healing from war and building resilience for the challenges ahead. We noticed who took the most leadership and spent more time with them. We listened for more ways we could be of use in the future. Mostly, we paid attention, weaving and strengthening this growing web of connections and support. We were present to people, and their stories and families and gifts. We loved, and we took in the love that was all around us. It was way less than what anybody deserved but it was all we had, and I have to believe that it was enough.

Demolition derby

I remember my first demolition derby, years ago as a young parent. It was the thrill of illicit activity that drew me there. My parents—middle-class academic types with progressive values—would never have dreamed of lending their support to such an uncouth spectacle; their disapproval would have been unconditional.

A theme of my adult life has been engaging with my parents' judgment and disapproval, throwing out any part that seemed rooted in fear or ignorance, testing whether I wanted to claim any of it as my own. I have sought out diversity. I love rubbing shoulders with my African American neighbors, with immigrants from Southeast Asia and West Africa, with other white folks who value this kind of community. For many years I worked with Italian and Irish-American Catholic moms, slowly building relationships in those close-knit ethnic neighborhoods. It makes me feel safer to not be so separated from people who are different from me. I can get to know human beings, and build some protection from the trap of believing that those differences are too great to be bridged.

Yet here, on the day of my second demolition derby, at the fairgrounds in a rural county, hours away from any big city, I realize how separated I still remain. This is an event that many locals look forward to all year. The road by the fairground is lined with cars and trucks, and the simple stands dug into the side of the hill are filled. Below us, eight old cars, windowless and battered beyond belief, are crashing into each other in a small enclosed place, vying to be the last one running.

With that first demolition derby, I went to face down my childhood. But I stayed for the excitement. This was a big, loud, outrageous world I had never even known existed. Just the fact that people were intentionally ramming into each other took my breath away. Then cars that looked like they could never move again, wheels askew or off entirely, back ends demolished, found a way to keep going, roaring in for another crash. At the end of the mayhem ordinary people stepped through what used to be the windshields of their mangled machines to accept the applause. We gasped and cheered. It was a totally memorable family outing. This time, with some idea of what to expect, and the illicit thrill factor less prominent, more of my attention was on the crowd.

We share a cabin in this county with six other families and have been coming up since before the boys were born. We know a lot about the land—our part of it in particular. We look forward to reading the weekly newspaper. With the chatty local columns on who has visited whom, 4H Club news, police blotter announcements of the occasional broken window or car accident, photos of proud hunters with their prize turkey or bear, we feel light years away from the big city.

Reading local news aloud to each other in the comfort of our cabin, however, is different from joining much of the county in person in their entertainment of choice. Surrounded by buzz cuts, cigarettes, tattoos, flags, and cars smashing into each other, I was definitely out of my element. My parents' disapproval hovered. Why waste so much energy on such needless destruction? What was the point? Surely people could find something more civilized, something *quieter* to watch.

But if I were taken to a popular local spectacle overseas, I would go with an attitude of respectful engagement—and that was the attitude I was interested in. These were my people, people I didn't have a chance to rub shoulders with on a daily basis, but people I needed to know and value if I would claim them as fellow Americans. These were people who worked in our forests, farms and factories, loved their children, did their best. I could get to know them, learn about their lives, their strengths, their dreams, the things that they—like my parents, like myself—feared and judged. Some of them I would surely love.

Some might even enjoy other kinds of entertainment as well. But this was where we were together right now. So, I gave thanks for the opportunity to be among neighbors I don't always remember I have, and entered into the spirit of demolition. A high point was watching a little green car in a heat of compacts. Not much to start with, it got smashed in more and more till it was unrecognizable as a vehicle. Yet every time we thought it was done for good, it reached deep and found wholly improbably new life, to not only move again, but go after other vehicles that still looked a little like cars. At the end, one of the last three still running, out the windshield opening came an unassuming young man, and we all gave a great cheer. It was good to be a witness to such skill, tenacity and enormous will to life, good to celebrate those qualities with my neighbors.

Bitter and sweet

Bitterness and sweet tears were on my mind this summer. On the eve of a five-day paddle down an unknown river early in the summer, we gathered for orientation at a campground on a Native reserve in Canada. Everything—and almost everybody— was new. We closed with an elder sharing stories from her grandmother, and one sentence settled deep into my heart with the ring of truth. Her grandmother had said, "You have to cry till your tears are sweet." Grieve beyond the point of bitterness.

Later, in the midst of a hard-fought national election, there was talk of "bitter voters" in our country. Politicians can try to sanitize that bitterness, or gloss over it, or pretend it is something that it is not. Or, much more problematic, they can feed on it for political advantage. But the advice of our native grandmother's grandmother—to cry till the tears are sweet— offers a way forward that rings with the sound of truth.

Yet how many of us just sneer at those who are drawn to the far right through a sense of betrayal and abandonment by the government and culture at large, those who cling stubbornly to fear and hate-mongering leaders?

In a liberal's attempt to scale this empathy wall, Arlie Hochschild explores the psyche of Louisiana Tea Party members in her book, *Strangers in Their Own Land*. She succeeds at evoking the feeling of what it's like to watch something that you have loved die—a bayou, the core of a small town, an industry that provided decent jobs, your hope for the future—then to try to endure, without making a show of grief, without asking for help.

She invites us to imagine waiting patiently in line for the American Dream. It lies just over the hill, but the line doesn't seem to be moving any more, and people are starting to cut in. "Strangers step ahead of you in line, making you anxious, resentful and afraid. A president allies with the line cutters, making you feel distrustful, betrayed. A person ahead of you in line insults you as an ignorant redneck, making you feel humiliated and mad. Economically, culturally, demographically, politically, you are suddenly a stranger in your own land."

A wise friend and ex-factory worker who is committed to dismantling the class system says that the heart of the project is learning to like each other. This is a tall order. There is much to be grieved, much to be overcome, much to be understood. I think again of Hochschild and her admonition that we can see what *they* can't see, but not what *we* can't see. Only by growing together toward one another will we gain the clarity and strength to name our common enemy and stand against the real evils that stalk our land and damage all our lives.

Bitterness is a hard, tight thing. It needs to be loosened, by attention, by understanding, by tears. There are so many lost hopes and broken promises. There is such a strong sense of betrayal, of becoming invisible in one's own country. How much deep and open-hearted listening will it take for the tears of the bitter voters to run sweet?

Reimagining men

There is a big soft spot in my heart for men. The warmth and welcome I received from three or four dads in my community growing up was like water in a parched land. The man who taught our Sunday School class when I was thirteen opened a rare and precious space by actually listening to what was on our hearts and minds. A male mentor saw what I was capable of as a young adult, and guided me toward a sense of self-worth and a life of meaning. I have an unfailingly loving and supportive partner and many dear male friends. I will never be confused about the goodness that can be found in men.

That said, it's hard to see so many men behaving so badly, and to see them so lost as a group. It is heartbreaking to take in the damage that has been done by men wielding power. As their right to behave badly is being increasingly called out, it is painful to watch the fear that such a challenge evokes.

The training in entitlement runs deep. So many men believe that they have a right to have their way, and that behaving like jerks with women is the natural order of things. Their outrage at a challenge to the assumptions that are at the core of their very identity is understandable. They are facing the unimaginable prospect of losing the only world they know, the world that has always been theirs.

Recent challenges to men's right to behave badly (the right of white men in positions of power most particularly) follow a whole series of attacks on their status. Their "natural right" to be in charge of our country is being attacked on all sides. Black people are just not staying down, despite the best efforts of Jim Crow and mass incarceration. The tide of immigrants of color is seemingly unstoppable. And now the women—including white women who "should" be standing at their sides—are starting to turn against them.

As their control is increasingly challenged, it's not surprising that the response is to hold on more tightly. Don't we all do that when we feel we might lose our grip? So, we see men in positions of power and privilege ready to sacrifice their brothers as they try desperately to hang on to every bit of control within their reach.

It's not easy to see the good in such men. Yet it has to be true that there's a place for every human being in the world we seek. We were all born good and innocent, openhearted and reaching for connection. Society has played a cruel trick on our men, training them in the ways of power while cutting off avenues for real closeness. It's only within this context that we can begin to understand the little boy longings that get played out so disastrously in grown men. To understand is not to excuse, of course, and certainly not to condone, but perhaps we can reach for some kindness as we stand up to unacceptable behavior.

I see an opportunity here for women to claim a much bigger power than we may ever have dreamed possible. There is real danger in setting our sights too low, and seeing victory in getting lured into traditionally male positions of power. Do we really want to take on male patterns of behavior in the name of liberation? Our vision for ourselves has to be much more encompassing.

Nobody will win by women following the men. We have to be in the lead. We have to see right through the entitlement, the unceasing quest for control, the reliance on violence, to the sweet little boys hidden deep inside. We have to stand up to their bad behavior without ever being confused about their innate goodness—and require them to change. In this scenario, everybody wins.

The con

I know about cons, have dealt with my share on the doorstep, been taken in once or twice, learned some of the signs. I remember one woman with an artful smile and a polished tale that needed just five transit tokens for a happy ending. I said I didn't believe a word of her story but offered a token in case the con covered real need.

But what about this man, this time? He's been on my doorstep before, asked for work or tokens to ride the bus. If this is a con, it is worn by a man who is also my neighbor.

What is the cost of trusting him? My good money could just go to drink — there is a whiff of that smell about him — and he would surely come back and ring my bell again. But there is a cost in not trusting him too — a separation between myself and his experience on the street.

I know how detail can coat a con and make it easier to swallow. Well, here's detail enough to drown in. The story he tells is about people who have fallen and are struggling to get back up, or have always been without in a system that makes life hard for the poor. It's a story of trying to land job interviews without a phone, get to the suburbs to work without cash up front for the bus, jump through the endless hoops set up by those who would help.

This story is true — but is it his? I wish I could be sure. I stand at the door and listen and listen, not wanting to be conned, hating my doubts. In the end I give him tokens and money. Even if it was all for drink, he has opened a window of truth, spoken with authority, told a story I need to hear. And the price of not trusting is just too high.

The view is not pretty through this window. I wonder how I would fare out there — how I would come to terms with a broken life, be thankful for systems that give something but not enough, hang on to dignity, wake up each day still clinging to hope. I don't like to think about it, would rather not look. Those of us on this side of the window are encouraged not to look all the time.

If this was a con at my door, it was a very little one — to draw me in, invite me to connection, play on my generosity. There are much bigger cons out there, cons with power and wealth and enormous seduction, cons that play not on our goodness, but on separation, fear and greed. There is the look-out-for-number-one individualism con, the pay-to-be-happy marketing con, the pay-to-live-risk-free insurance con, the pay-to-be-safe-from-enemies security con.

If I would choose to not be conned, then I need to choose it all the time. I need to look to the lies beyond my doorstep—the lies that saturate my consciousness and make me believe I have a right to freedom from this kind of discomfort. Besides, I think the man at my door was telling the truth.

Curiosity and respect

I picked up the book, *Respect*, because it was written by a woman who was one of the revered "big girls" from my childhood. In it was an unexpected gift: Sarah Lawrence-Lightfoot's suggestion that a critical element of respect is curiosity. Just the day after I put the book down, a colleague at work shared with me his experience of receiving admiring surprise at his ability to stand in for the boss at a radio interview. To this highly accomplished African American man, such surprised acclaim came across as subtle disrespect, part of the racism he deals with every day. When I mentioned Sarah's idea of curiosity as an element of respect, we realized that a response of wondering how he had become so good at that kind of thing would have been better received.

So what keeps us from this attitude of respectful curiosity? Our capacity to wonder is enormously disrespected when we are children, first by parents and others who tire of our questions and tend to pronounce from above rather than explore together, then by an educational system which prescribes what we should ask questions about and what the right answers are. Many of us are left deeply damaged in our ability to wonder about the things we don't know.

Some of us don't inquire because we doubt our capacity to

understand. It's like asking a question in a barely-mastered foreign language: you often get an answer that's way beyond your ability to comprehend. Or we don't want to admit what we don't know, since not revealing our curiosity can save us from humiliation. We may choose to not be curious about things that are painful. By not asking, we hope to shield ourselves from knowing, or shield others from feeling their pain. So not being curious becomes a protection, from showing ourselves too fully, or addressing things that are hard to face.

Wondering implies a desire for connection. It can be hard to be curious about things or people we feel no connection to. We don't have enough information (or have too much misinformation) to know what we might be genuinely curious about. Unchallenged, the smallness of our world can stifle curiosity.

There are also ways of being curious that are not respectful. Sometimes our questioning is like scratching an itch. We want to know because we'll feel better; we're not thinking about the other person at all. Or our motivation is an avid interest in ferreting out information that can be used to pursue a goal, or to judge or categorize. If I want to know your opinion so I can choose whether to be friends or enemies, if I ask your credentials so I can decide whether you are worthy, then I'm not really interested in you, not curious about you as a person. The genuinely curious question would be the one that helps me understand how you tick.

There is a more subtle kind of limited curiosity. It may be fine, for example, for a white person to wonder how black people do their hair. But if I ask a specific person just because they're handy, they become a means to an end. I'm not being fully present with them at that moment. I need to be genuinely curious about that particular person in that moment in order to convey respect.

Being curious is a wonderful way to get to know people. I

love to listen to people talk about their work. If I ask enough questions, I always hit pay dirt. I often get a glimpse into a world I never would have known, and I always discover a passion or a skill or a commonality that draws me closer to that person.

When you're being curious you can't be judgmental, because there are no right answers. The other person is the expert, the resourceful one. Genuine curiosity is open-ended, relational, rooted in the present moment. Sarah from my childhood was right. Generous, open-hearted deep curiosity inevitably conveys respect.

5. Hardship and Hope

Blowing on coals

When I was a little girl, I loved reading stories about the old days in this country. They always made me appreciate basic things I took for granted—like heat and warmth and light. In a world without matches, keeping the fire going was so important. In more than one of these stories, a child in a family whose fire had gone out had the job of getting a shovelful of coals from the neighbors. I could feel the urgency of the mission, the sense of responsibility, as a child carefully guarded the glowing coals, on a trip through a snowy night, bringing warmth and light and energy back to a home grown cold and dark.

The stories of banking the fire at night are less dramatic, but in a way more compelling. To conserve on wood, they would cover the fire, reducing the flow of air, so that it would burn very slowly through the night. In the morning it might seem dead, but when some hardy early riser uncovered the coals and blew and blew, some of those coals would begin to glow. With enough blowing, they grew hot enough to set a bit of tinder alight—and the fire was once again alive, ready to provide heat and light.

This blowing on coals evokes mystery and magic. It is an act of faith and of power. We don't have the capacity to create life where there is none, yet we can uncover the heart of something that seemed cold, and literally breathe it back into life. Sometimes it takes the littlest puff, sometimes just one good hard blow. Other times, ash blows in your eyes, you get red in the face, and you wonder if your lungs are going to burst. But what a glow of satisfaction when that first little flame jumps out!

There is something about coals that calls to me. They are so warm, so ready. I've been wondering if that's part of what we're in this world to do—to have an eye out for the places around us where no fire is visible, but the coals still have life, and to be willing to blow. We can help ease away the overlay of uncaring, the dead covering of fear and discouragement. We can breathe out our hope, love and confidence in that person or that situation. We can get in close, inhale deeply, and give it our all. What would happen in this world if all those banked fires—in hearts and programs and communities—could burst into open flame?

Of course there are times when the fire has gone all the way out, when we left it too long or something unexpected happened and there is no life left in the coals. That's the time to put on a warm coat, get out the shovel and bucket, and give thanks that we have neighbors.

The gift

Building on dual passions, for urban agriculture and for connections across barriers that divide us, I joined the board of a local urban farming project years ago. The farm, then a white-led initiative in a black neighborhood, was full of everything that is right and everything that is wrong in our society. It has been a rich and wonderful experience, and nothing about it has been easy.

As we struggled with the problems of any small non-profit, with scarcity on all fronts, we also found ourselves dealing with gut-wrenching staff issues centered around gender and race, all within the context of an unfulfilled vision of local leadership, and ever-present second-guessing about the appropriateness of white people like me being involved at all.

I had to look hard at the ugliness of racism as it affected all of us in so many ways. Several years in, I found myself leading the board because no one else would do it, and we all knew I could. I felt the weight of the farm's survival heavy on my shoulders as I tried to nurture new board members and staff of color, follow the leadership that was there, and hold everything together in the face of unrelenting challenges.

Our commitment to grounding the farm back in its neighborhood led to a shared decision a few years ago to not make a new administrative hire till we could hire locally, which led to more work for our one farmer, greater burden on the few remaining board members, and an increasingly stressed context for both program work and fundraising.

We've done amazingly well under the circumstances, made good decisions, survived. The potential remains enormous and I've never regretted the choice to put so much time and energy into nurturing this jewel of an urban farm. I've loved being around all the people who love it, and have known that it was a gift in my life. One fellow board member, who clearly values me but just doesn't reassure or comfort my whiteness, has shone a light on parts of me that might otherwise have gone unexamined. It just would have been so much easier if I'd looked away and settled for smaller challenges!

Months ago, there was a turnaround — with new local board members of color, some very successful grant-writing, and a vision on the part of our new board leader to transform to a cooperative model. That first newly-expanded and energized board meeting brought more unexpected emotional work for me. Now, rather than feeling overwhelmed by just trying to keep the farm afloat, I was overwhelmed by feelings that I was no longer needed — clearly the wrong color, in the wrong place.

I fought my way, slowly and painfully, to the perspective that it's not my job to act preemptively on the assumption that I'm not welcome, even if I'm white, even if it would feel easier to give up and disappear. It's not mine to make assumptions about how others perceive me. That's their job. My job is to keep showing up as fully as I know how, despite my feelings, and to let others take the lead in evaluating my contribution and working out the racial composition of the board going forward. At some point, everything I'm doing now may well be adequately and more appropriately done by others, but I can still be fully present till then. I can continue to treasure the relationships that have been built through struggle over the years. I can even make new ones.

In the midst of all this hard work — emotional and otherwise — I had the opportunity to support a young climate activist friend. His vision, commitment and initiative had put him in the center of the national climate movement, with all its contentious issues around turf, leadership, and direction, and with opportunities to make race-related mistakes at every turn. He was engaged in a delicate racially-charged alliance-building project and glad for the opportunity to get some attention.

What became abundantly clear was that living through the challenges in my own little corner of the world had set me up to understand experientially the challenges he was dealing with. By bringing my own hard-won experience to the table, knowing in my bones something of what he was going through, he could rest in feeling seen and understood. He could use the space I was able to offer to look at his hardest feelings, regain perspective and think freshly about next steps. As I stretched to bring everything I had to support this man I loved, doing work that mattered deeply to me, I was thankful beyond words for the gifts I had been given by the farm.

Leaving the Land of I

It didn't take a Kansas tornado for us to find ourselves in the Land of I. Many of us were born there and have lived there all our lives, not knowing any other place as home. For others, our homeland has been transformed so gradually that it's been hard to notice the change from day to day. Yet here each one of us is, surrounded by all the bright colors and the glittering promises.

All I have to do to be happy in the Land of I is to make the right choices among all the possibilities and opportunities that are flashing so insistently around me. What products will give me satisfaction, pleasure and status? What clothing will show me off to best advantage? What amusements will entertain? What friends will best fulfill my needs? What education will lead to the most satisfying career? What family will enhance my happiness? What choices will maximize my power and influence? Even, what good works can I undertake to fulfill my urge toward generosity and compassion?

If I choose well, I can have a good life and perhaps leave my mark on the world. If I stumble, I can correct and make a better selection. If I fall, I can hope for the strength to get up and try again. If I continue to struggle, it is because too many of my choices have been unwise.

In the Land of I, every person also gets a pair of rose-colored glasses—to make the colors and the promises more seductive, and to obscure the hard realities that nobody really wants to look at anyway. Immersed in the bustle and hype of the Land of I, it's hard to imagine any other world. Yet one is there and available to all of us, just a click of the heels away.

This world is quieter. The choices are less insistent. The lights flash less, but burn more steadily. Rose-colored glasses are nowhere to be found, and we see things happening to others around us that make us grieve. There are still individual choices, but they are more subtle. How is my life entwined with those around me at this moment—and the next—and what attitude can I hold, what step can I take that will increase our overall welfare? In the longer term, how can I orient and equip myself to make my best and fullest contribution to this world, and how can I help others to do the same?

No longer in the Land of I, we don't have to make all these choices on our own. In this world, others don't care so much about the glitter of our clothes or social circles or careers, but they are deeply invested in promoting our gifts, our goodness and our potential.

None of us have to abandon our own center to live here; rather we all get to inhabit it more fully as each person finds a place in the middle of ever-greater circles of "we." We get to be for ourselves and for others at the same time. But first we have to make the decision to leave the Land of I. If we can take off those rose-colored glasses, turn our backs on the glitter and the empty promises and start claiming our connections, together we can find our way back home.

Microorganisms and fertility

There's something about the earth that calls to me. I love the feel of a good rich soil, knowing how it nourishes the plants we need in order to live. I love making compost, finding earthworms, breaking up clumps of earth with my hands to create a bed for new seeds. So, it's been thrilling to read a book that links the fertility of our soil with our wealth. At one point it talks about all the millions of microorganisms in every little bit of good soil. Those microorganisms have never gotten much respect. Scientists have been much more interested in how adding fertilizers—along with pesticides to kill the bugs that grow on the plants—can produce increased yields. But they also know that after a while, you have to add more fertilizers to get an increase, and then you have to add even more to maintain that yield, and then, even with such high dosages, crop yields start to decline.

Why? It seems that all those fertilizers and pesticides kill off the microorganisms, so you end up with the soil as a sterile medium, useful only for receiving outside inputs and physically holding up the plants. For some reason, that's just not enough to make them thrive. Nobody seems to know exactly what all those microorganisms are and how they all work together, but it turns out that they're critical to the fertility of the soil.

46

Well, this got me thinking. None of those microorganisms make the difference by themselves. But that big community all working together creates something of enormous value. It reminds me of human communities, creating culture, creating wealth, creating a fertile place for people to thrive. But I worry that we're losing our fertility. The external inputs that seemed so hopeful when they were first introduced—the consumer products, the commercial entertainment, the advertising—are killing off the vitality of our soil. For a while it seemed like more inputs led to increased well-being, but as the doses got heavier, the rate of increase in quality of life slowed down, and now, despite continued, ever more feverish expansion of external inputs, our well-being is steadily declining.

The loss of good soil is a serious problem; it's hard to even get one's mind around the world-wide implications for feeding our planet in the face of such degradation. But I find reason for hope in my compost pile. It's not impossible to create good soil. It's not impossible to nurture the conditions that allow those microorganisms to find each other and start working their magic together again.

Similarly, I think we need to take ourselves very seriously as the microorganisms of society. We don't have to accept our communities becoming an ever-more sterile medium into which ever-increasing doses of mass culture are necessary to prop up our ever-more-uniform lives. We can build up our resistance to those outside inputs, which are poisoning the soil of our communities. We can put our energies to interacting with each other and creating richness from that interaction. The process remains a mysterious one. We may not know exactly how it happens, but it seems to be true that we, working together, with each other, are the only hope for a renewed fertility of our degraded culture.

Balance

Who doesn't love watching people who can keep their balance in seemingly impossible situations? I think of gymnasts who do amazing feats on a balance bar, ice-skaters who leap and land with stunning grace, surfers who stay upright in the face of giant crashing waves.

So many forces in today's world conspire to knock us off balance. The news seems designed to keep us in a constant state of upset. We reach frantically for some kind of mental/emotional equilibrium, get a precarious hold, then someone does or says the next unbelievably outrageous thing, and we're off balance again.

It's like being caught in the big waves at the beach when you don't have the skill to ride them. They knock you down and carry you crashing to the shore, leaving you battered, bruised and abraded. You get up, gather yourself together, determine to go back in, and are knocked down again by that overwhelming relentless force.

I remember how terrified I was of those waves when our family used to camp by the ocean when I was small. I would spend hours close by our tent, making designs in the sand with shells and rocks — small objects over which I had some control. It wasn't until adulthood that I learned how to manage in those waves — getting far enough out that I could go down under just as one was ready to crash, then come up to calm on the other side.

How could we find a similar strategy with those relentless waves of bad news? What would it mean to stay in the water, but not take the full brunt of those breakers, not get continually body-slammed into the sand (and without taking the easier route of limiting our news intake to the calmer waters of sports, fashion or movies)? I actually wonder if the breakers are a distraction, and the real issues are to be found in deeper water.

The elements of such a strategy might include keeping a judicious distance from much of what is presented as "news" but is really just fear mongering; having places to take our outrage and heartbreak; and being very discriminating and proactive about how, when, from what sources, and in what dosages we take in the information we need in order to stay engaged. The world badly needs us upright, breathing, in touch with our love, and intact. Putting thought, time and energy into developing a practice and discipline around the news that works for us is a project well worth taking on.

Then there is the question of how to handle the individuals who knock us off balance—those who are insufferably clueless and say the most outrageous things; those who wield power at high cost to others; the ones whose storms and personal drama engulf everyone in their orbit; those who have that uncanny capacity to leave us questioning our worth. We all have developed a variety of responses: fighting back with equal force; joining our outrage with others so we feel less alone; or just keeping our distance, as I did from the surf as a child.

But I think there's a different and much more powerful response here that's similar to staying in the water and going under the waves in a high surf. A thought that a friend shared months ago continues to reverberate in my mind: If we can find a way to bring them deep inside us, into our hearts, they can't knock us off balance. The physics is unassailable; you can't be rocked from inside. The practice, however, is quite another thing. It seems like a super-human task to find our way to such a place.

Yet the need for keeping our balance in this world is compelling. And I think the gymnasts and skaters and surfers can point a way forward. None of them could stay balanced at the beginning. Their ability in the present is the result of a clear vision of a highly-prized goal, determination, and tons of practice. They worked day in and day out to get to the point where they didn't fall, where they didn't get knocked off balance, where they could be and do what they held in their mind's eye.

6. Peril and Possibility

Imagining a new thing

It is easier to imagine the end of life on earth than a new economic system — a lethal failure of the imagination. I am still stunned by the truth, and horror, of this statement. Our growth-driven economic system is leading us toward environmental destruction, yet we'll go along with this nightmare, simply for lack of imagination. It gives me a new perspective on the people who believe in rapture and the end days. If you are a good person trying to do the right thing, yet everything around you seems to be falling apart, it may be easier to imagine the end days than any change here on earth. And if you are around passionate people with vivid imaginations who paint a compelling picture of how the rapture will play out, it becomes that much easier to believe.

Yet people have been prophesying imminent apocalypse for well over 2000 years, and I'm much more interested in life here on earth. So I'd rather imagine a new economic system instead, and paint a different picture that's equally passionate and compelling.

Fortunately, it's not that hard. There are lots of people all over the world — including economists — who are busily engaged in imagining a new thing, and there is a growing consensus about many of its elements: a reorientation from a focus on producing money to a focus on producing goods that people need; measuring our economic health not by the sum of all economic activity, good, bad or indifferent, but by how well people are doing; moving from growth in consumption and scale to growth in knowledge, technical ability and flexible intelligence; production methods that move beyond waste, so that by-products of one process become valued inputs somewhere else; a regulatory and tax system that works toward equity; an emphasis on the value of community and caring, and local ability to produce wealth and meet human needs.

Yes, yes, you may say, that all sounds very good, but it will never happen. I would quote, in return, the wise person who said that despair is an insult to the future. And, anyhow, where does despair get us besides what our current society has to offer— endless consumption and entertainment, or individualized pursuit of a private good life, or embracing the rapture? At least the work of imagining, both what could be and how it might come to pass, provides some meaning.

It isn't work that's easy. The institutions and powers that seem to have society in thrall, moving us inevitably toward destruction, are immense. The financial markets blatantly protect their power and greed. Politics is increasingly devoid of civility or cooperation. The solutions the system creates for the problems it has produced just seem to breed bigger problems— all at the expense of the environment. If this is all we focus on when we look out, the end days could easily be right over the horizon.

I'm helped here by a concept I came across from theologian Walter Wink, that every human institution has a divine vocation. They may have strayed from that vocation, but it is still there to be found. Politics has a vocation of providing a structure that allows people to live together. Economics has a vocation of creating a way for people to meet their needs. It is our job to call our institutions back to their divine vocation. If we can choose this role, of imagining what our institutions are really there to do, and calling them home, we will find ourselves in a new place of power and authority.

The times call out for us to imagine the future as if our life, as if all life on earth, depended on it. But we can choose a different, even more compelling, motivation—and engage in this work because imagining a new thing is at the very heart of what it means to be human.

Risk management

As I was biking into a poorer neighborhood just west of mine to get to my local YMCA, I noticed how the number of bikers without helmets grew, and couldn't help but think of my recent time in Africa, the tons of bike riders there, and the total non-existence of helmets. I think most of us would identify an arc of progress here: Africa in the rear, many in the US ahead of them, my helmet-conscious neighborhood in the vanguard.

There's logic in this line of reasoning. Historically, prosperity has created the conditions for risk mitigation, with generally good results. It's great to ensure that water is safe to drink, require people to follow traffic laws, and encourage vaccination against deadly and contagious diseases.

As we extend from these overall public protections, however, there are some troubling trends. We seem to be focusing more and more on consumer behavior, product safety and prohibitions against individual behavior that is deemed risky. In a society with great income inequality, such risk mitigation comes at a price that is often paid individually. The more affluent can drive the biggest and safest cars, consume the best health care, and buy protection from violence in gated communities. People with fewer resources have fewer options about the risks they are exposed to, from the environmental contaminants in their neighborhoods to the lack of spending money for "extras" like bike helmets.

We have identified so many more behaviors as risky than our parents or grandparents ever did. Yet, in a crusade to use our resources and well-developed risk management capacity to eliminate risk, the expense of additional protection yields less and less additional well-being. I would go farther, and suggest that we may have reached the point where our risk aversion is putting us in greater danger.

Childhood asthma, for example, has now been linked with the reduction in gut bacteria that comes with use of antibiotics in the first years of life. I have to wonder: are those parents who are trying hardest to protect their young children from bacterial infections actually putting them at greater risk? The early childhood education field is struggling more and more with this paradox. The regulations around sanitizing, that are becoming increasingly stringent in an effort to create germ-free environments for our little ones, are creating their own unintentional hazards—both in the dangers of inhaling/ingesting the sanitizing agents, and in the decreased opportunities for children to acquire their own antibodies to fight off infection.

Looking through the widest possible lens, by far the greatest risk we are facing as a species is the threat to life on earth that comes from global warming. From that perspective, our focus for risk mitigation is seriously misplaced. Those of us with the largest carbon footprint—driving cars, heating and cooling big houses, eating food that's traveled thousands of miles, mindlessly consuming products that depend on scarce natural resources—are engaging in the most risky behavior of all. Riding without a bike helmet entails risk. Pursuing consumption and economic growth at the cost of the planet's integrity, however, is a whole different order of risk.

I wonder if part of our obsession with fighting germs and pursuing bike safety is a manifestation of this paradox. An immediate risk that we have means to address feels more real than those larger ones that seem so distant and out of reach. And, while taking antibiotics and wearing bike helmets can't protect us from climate change, at least it's something that we as individuals can do to feel safer.

I'm not advocating that we stop taking basic safety precautions or that we intentionally put our loved ones in danger. But what if, whenever we spent time, attention, money or energy in order to feel safer ourselves, we committed to spending an equal amount of time, attention, money or energy to reduce the risk that our cumulative individual and societal decisions are bringing to others in far-away places or future generations?

As I think about this whole issue, a couple of lessons stand out. First, it always helps to step back and take a look at the big picture. Second, when we think about risk management, it may be time to look beyond traditional technical and regulatory solutions—to mass movements for changed priorities, perhaps. Finally, a little humility may be in order. Those countries in Africa that have lots of helmet-less bike riders and few cars to hit them—that seem so backward to us—may be engaging in much less risky behavior overall than our own rich industrialized fossil-fueled hyper-risk-averse societies.

Extract or generate?

When people talk about our economic system, the traditional language is about free markets, free enterprise, free trade, the invisible hand, the profit motive, supply and demand. Critics use different—and often stronger—language: runaway capitalism, profiteering, unbridled greed, systemic inequality, corporate control. But until recently, I'd never heard our economy characterized as "extractive," and that term has gotten me thinking.

There's something about it that rings very true. We pride ourselves on the quantity of riches that we can extract from beneath the earth's crust. We extract maximum value from the topsoil and the forests and the oceans. Employers typically have a goal of extracting ever more work from their employees. Financial institutions prosper when they extract maximum profit from every transaction—ATM withdrawals, credit card charges, mortgage rates, currency exchange interactions, and things most of us don't even understand, like credit swaps, hedges and derivatives. The goal in each case is maximum extraction for maximum profit. The losers from all of this extraction, clearly, are ordinary people, the earth, and other living things.

The alternative could be characterized as a "generative"

economy. I looked this word up to make sure I knew what it meant "having the power or function of generating, originating, producing, creating." Where there wasn't anything before, there is now something new.

Generative. My mind goes immediately to the soil. I was picking lettuce not long ago, getting ready to make a lunch for work, and noticed a little dirt at the base of a leaf. I rubbed it off, but didn't even bother to wash it. After all, that was dirt that had been created in my compost pile, and I knew all the good ingredients that had gone into it. I love generating soil for my garden. There is some necessary extraction of nutrients from the soil as the plants grow, but with compost continually added, it just keeps getting richer and richer. Overall, my little agricultural system is far more generative than extractive.

There are many other places in our lives where this distinction might apply. I think of extracting productivity from those who work under us, as opposed to generating loyalty and trust. I think of extracting obedience from children, as opposed to generating a spirit of mutual cooperation. I think of extracting the benefits of a nice neighborhood or a well-functioning religious congregation for oneself, as opposed to putting energy into generating benefits for others. I think of extracting entertainment from an outside source as opposed to generating fun for oneself and others. I think of extracting the maximum value out of any exchange, as opposed to focusing on the opportunity it brings to generate new possibilities or relationships.

I'm deeply committed to building the power and the will to challenge our extractive economy, from curbing fossil fuel extraction to taming multinational corporations to taxing speculative financial transactions that maximize profit at the expense of our community well-being. I'm also committed to supporting new economic institutions that help build up a generative economy—coops of all kinds; credit unions;

community gardens; enterprises that embrace the triple bottom line of profit, people, and planet; initiatives of the Transition movement.

As I continue to find and expand my place in such efforts, however, I don't have to wait. At the same time, I can consider my own life choices. I can notice where I am extracting as a citizen, family member, worker and consumer — and where I am generating new wealth, resources and possibilities. As I notice, I can shift my weight toward a generative economy.

What we protect

We are a fiercely protective species. We seem to be hardwired to protect ourselves, in a biological imperative to fight or flight. When external circumstances keep men from protecting their families, their very souls are damaged. Gentle mothers become fierce when the safety of their children is at stake. We can be called to gladly protect our nation, even at risk of our lives, to the extent that there is a strong sense of common identity. We protect what we feel to be ours, based on our love and our sense of connection.

If we tend to protect that which we claim as ours, then there is a natural corollary. We don't have as strong an urge to protect that which we can't tell is of us, which we can't feel that we love. Racism, classism and religious/ethnic divisions separate us from others. We see people on the street or hear about them in the news, and think of them as "other." Sometimes the separation comes from simple and innocent lack of contact. Sometimes it is deliberately fanned by those who have an agenda that is served by separation. But the result is the same: they are no longer "of us," they are not ours to love and protect.

This dynamic plays out with our Earth as well. The dominant frame for relating to the environment over the last several centuries has been one of gaining mastery over it, and integral to that quest is a clear separation between us and the rest of the natural world. By definition, this is a conflicted relationship; if we come out on top, the rest of the environment comes out underneath. Since we see ourselves as smarter and more powerful, we are comfortable being in charge, and reaping the benefits of exploitation. The material world is at our disposal to use—and use up—in any way that serves our perceived interests. The underlying assumptions are the same as those of slaveholding.

A second frame, of stewardship of the environment, is more nuanced. A steward, says the dictionary, is one who manages another's affairs, usually with their best interest in mind. The relationship is not inherently conflicted, as it is with mastery; stewards of the earth are more likely to put effort into caring for it. But the separation remains. As a steward, I act not on my behalf, but on behalf of another—and the assumption lingers that the steward knows best. Slaveholders who considered themselves enlightened may well have embraced the concept of stewardship of their property.

If our goal is to protect the environment, then we'll certainly have to give up the frame of mastery and everything that goes with it—domination, control, warfare and subjection. But stewardship, with its tone of caring for a separate other, won't quite get us there either. The end point has to be reclaiming our connection with and belonging to the Earth. Just as our families and our people are part of the larger body that we claim as ours, so are we part of an even larger body, the biosphere. When we can know this truth deep in our bones, then the Earth becomes ours—to connect with, to love fiercely, and to protect.

Big enough

I was having one of my—not uncommon—moments of feeling just too little. The world was looking pretty bleak and its problems pretty big. Economic inequality, racism, climate change—how could I possibly hope to make any difference in the face of enormous forces like these?

A friend was listening to me, and as I shared my sense of helplessness and hopelessness, my wish to not even turn my head in the direction of these big painful wrongs that I could do nothing about, I was able to hear myself in a new way. I sounded like a very little girl. The voice inside me that was speaking was a voice from my childhood.

It makes perfect sense. I was too little then. The forces that governed my life were way beyond my control. I saw the things that weren't working right—for me, for my family—and had no way of making them better. In my particular situation, I didn't even see a way to complain. So I did my best, learned my own set of survival skills, put my head down, and found my way, for better or for worse, into adulthood.

Now this isn't to say that my life has been bleak. Far from it. I've experienced love in a variety of wonderful forms, found many meaningful ways to spend my time, gotten pleasure from the talents of countless people on this earth, been nurtured by the richness of the natural world. As an adult, I've discovered that I'm not helpless, that I can make things happen in the circles around me. I've continued to look for ways to address these big evils, but through all those years I've still carried that image of myself as just not big enough.

I remember my pivotal "aha moment" about the relationship between the climate emergency and despair: the feelings of despair that come up so quickly around climate change are not new. Those feelings were with us long before we had ever imagined the possibility of the end of life on earth as we know it. They are old feelings from our childhood—when things were that scary, and we felt that small. I find the concept so refreshing: the feelings of despair that come up in the face of climate change are not inevitable. They are ours to change. The current situation is just an irresistible magnet for those old fears—which are always looking for a convenient place to attach in the present.

This is certainly not to say that we don't have a problem, or that the challenges we face are insignificant. As the big international forces that have brought us to this point grow in their interconnections and global impact, the threats are immense, immediate, and dire. But what if we are big enough?

I'm helped by recognizing a similar trajectory behind climate change, economic inequality and racism. It starts with the combined assumption of separation and goal of mastery— in relation to both other human beings and the environment. Those who have more justify their right to it, then they work to protect what they have. This attitude lead to injustice and trauma on a massive scale—for both people and the earth. The systems that have been built on these foundations are enormous and complex, but underlying them are human dynamics that can be understood, faced and changed. Systems that have been built can be dismantled, and people who have done damage and been damaged can be healed.

What if this is just the right sized challenge for grown-ups like us? What if each of us gets to be our own full loving human self in relation to these big issues? What if we assumed that we were big enough? Big enough to look at what's wrong; to understand; to say what we think; to apply what we know to our personal choices; to engage with our friends, colleagues and neighbors, and gather others around good programs; to be players on the public stage?

In the process, we'll have to get good at teasing out the sticky old voices of despair from the reality of interesting and important challenges in the present. Those voices from our childhood may be the biggest thing that's holding back our world. It was true back then: we were too little. What good news that we're now big enough!

Serenity

God grant me the serenity to accept the things I cannot change;
courage to change the things I can; and wisdom to know the difference.
I've always liked this advice, but recently I've found myself
wondering about the overlap between serenity and resignation.
Some things are clearly and simply unchangeable. The sky can
be gray. Winter follows fall. Loss is painful—and deep loss is
deeply painful. We all age. Accidents happen. We can't change
these things, yet some may require courage to face, and our
greatest peace will come from facing the hard parts square on.

Desmond Tutu has spoken powerfully about the past as
unchangeable "There can be no peace without reconciliation,
no reconciliation without forgiveness, no forgiveness without
giving up all hope for a better past." How can we accept the past
serenely, without projecting it into the present and the future?
There are historic realities that need to be acknowledged,
possibly with serenity. People who have been hurt themselves,
for example, often hurt others. The tendrils of the past do
indeed entangle us. But there is courage involved in imagining
the possibility that the chain can be broken. Although there
are good reasons why I resigned myself early to a life of lonely
self-sufficiency, that resignation does not serve me well in the
present, and I have to believe I can change.

Other things seem unchangeable because they are so big.
Racism has dug its roots deep into society, pervading and
degrading everyone's life. Our economic system, based on
greed, no longer serves the well-being of our communities. Big-
power foreign policy distorts the priorities of smaller countries
all over the world. Climate change disproportionately impacts
the poor. Our culture is debased by a relentless focus on sex,
violence, novelty and consumption.

Do we accept these realities with serenity? Acceptance might
seem easier to live with than a sense of failure, frustration or
outrage; and constantly railing against things that are too big to

change certainly does not make for a life of grace.

Yet they are not right, and I just can't see accepting them serenely. Rather than tucking them away out of sight, as unfortunate but unchangeable, somehow we need to hold them clearly in front of us. Our attention may not be on them all the time, but if they are in our sight, if we have decided that we care, if we have a vision of how we wish things to be different, then opportunities will present themselves. We will make a different choice about a conversation, or a friend, or a purchase, or the use of an evening, or even the thoughts inside our head. We will turn our lives in the direction of what we long for in this world—and things will change.

Ultimately, I do believe that we need the wisdom to know the difference. Let's reach for serenity in the face of the truly unchangeable. But let's also assume that much of what we face in the present, both inside of us and in the world all around, is full of the seeds of change, just calling for more imagination and courage than we know we have.

Also in this series

Quaker Roots and Branches
John Lampen

Quaker Roots and Branches explores what Quakers call their 'testimonies' – the interaction of inspiration, faith and action to bring change in the world. It looks at Quaker concerns around the sustainability of the planet, peace and war, punishment, and music and the arts in the past and today. It stresses the continuity of their witness over three hundred and sixty-five years as well as their openness to change and development.

Telling the Truth about God
Rhiannon Grant

Telling the truth about God without excluding anyone is a challenge to the Quaker community. Drawing on the author's academic research into Quaker uses of religious language and her teaching to Quaker and academic groups, Rhiannon Grant aims to make accessible some key theological and philosophical insights. She explains that Quakers might sound vague but are actually making clear and creative theological claims.

What Do Quakers Believe?
Geoffrey Durham

Geoffrey Durham answers the crucial question 'What do Quakers believe?' clearly, straightforwardly and without jargon. In the process he introduces a unique religious group whose impact and influence in the world is far greater than their numbers suggest. *What Do Quakers Believe?* is a friendly, direct and accessible toe-in-the-water book for readers who have often wondered who these Quakers are, but have never quite found out.

CHRISTIAN ALTERNATIVE
BOOKS

THE NEW OPEN SPACES

Throughout the two thousand years of Christian tradition there
have been, and still are, groups and individuals that exist in
the margins and upon the edge of faith. But in Christianity's
contrapuntal history it has often been these outcasts and
pioneers that have forged contemporary orthodoxy out
of former radicalism as belief evolves to engage with and
encompass the ever-changing social and scientific realities. Real
faith lies not in the comfortable certainties of the Orthodox,
but somewhere in a half-glimpsed hinterland on the dirt track
to Emmaus, where the Death of God meets the Resurrection,
where the supernatural Christ meets the historical Jesus,
and where the revolution liberates both the oppressed and
the oppressors.

Welcome to Christian Alternative... a space at the edge where
the light shines through.
If you have enjoyed this book, why not tell other readers by
posting a review on your preferred book site.

Christian Atheist
Belonging without Believing
Brian Mountford
Christian Atheists don't believe in God but miss him: especially
the transcendent beauty of his music, language, ethics, and
community.
Paperback: 978-1-84694-439-0 ebook: 978-1-84694-929-6

Compassion Or Apocalypse?
A Comprehensible Guide to the Thoughts of René Girard
James Warren
How René Girard changes the way we think about God and the
Bible, and its relevance for our apocalypse-threatened world.
Paperback: 978-1-78279-073-0 ebook: 978-1-78279-072-3

Diary Of A Gay Priest
The Tightrope Walker
Rev. Dr. Malcolm Johnson
Full of anecdotes and amusing stories, but the Church is still a
dangerous place for a gay priest.
Paperback: 978-1-78279-002-0 ebook: 978-1-78099-999-9

Do You Need God?
Exploring Different Paths to Spirituality Even For Atheists
Rory J.Q. Barnes
An unbiased guide to the building blocks of spiritual belief.
Paperback: 978-1-78279-380-9 ebook: 978-1-78279-379-3

Readers of ebooks can buy or view any of these bestsellers by clicking on the live link in the title. Most titles are published in paperback and as an ebook. Paperbacks are available in traditional bookshops. Both print and ebook formats are available online.

Find more titles and sign up to our readers' newsletter at
http://www.johnhuntpublishing.com/christianity
Follow us on Facebook at
https://www.facebook.com/ChristianAlternative